AF486658

Wanderers

poems & illustrations

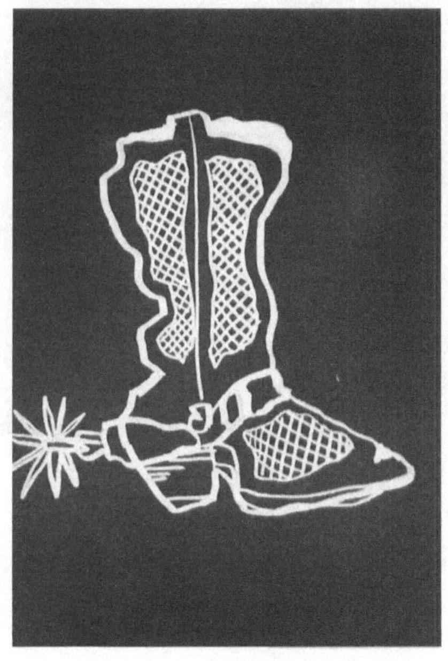

Linzi Garcia and Deon Morrow

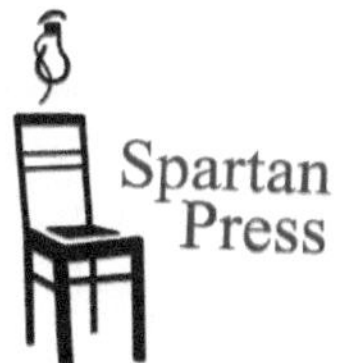

Spartan Press

Spartan Press
Kansas City, MO
spartanpresskc@gmail.com

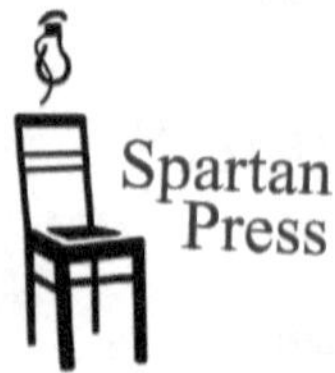

Spartan
Press

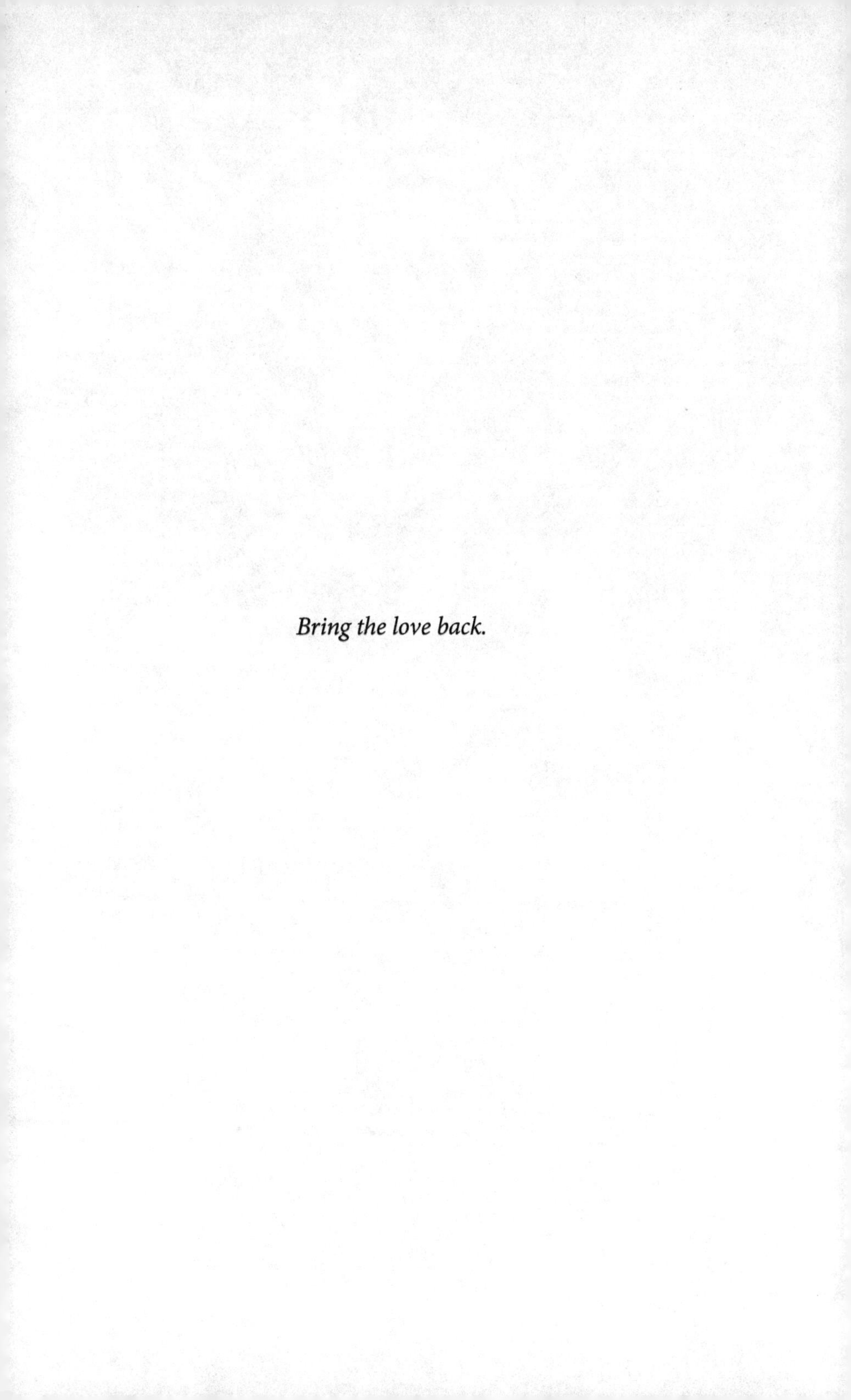

Bring the love back.

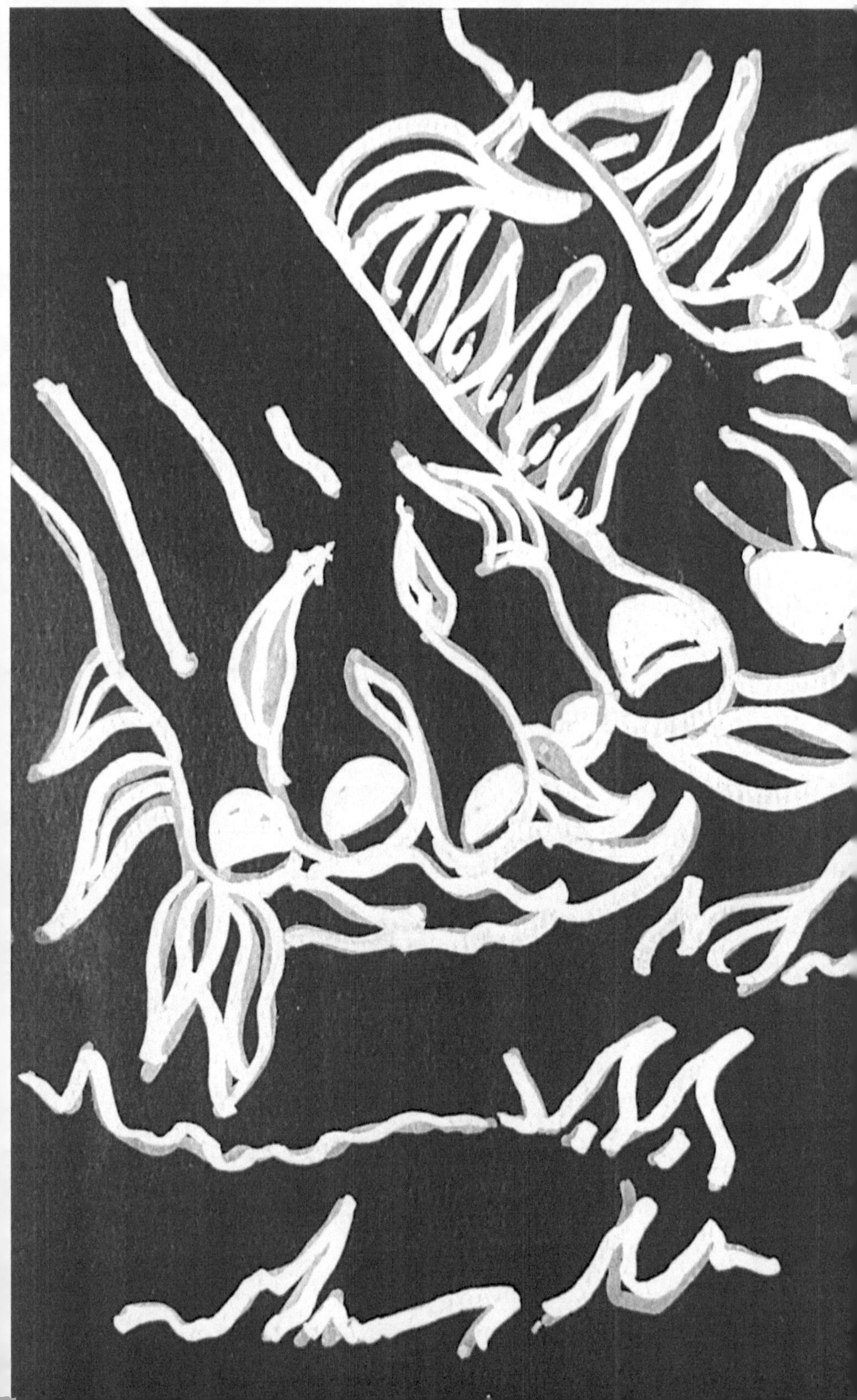

On the wildflower walk,
grass seeds get stuck
between my toes.
Watch out
for the cockleburs–
their bite
worse than the tick's.

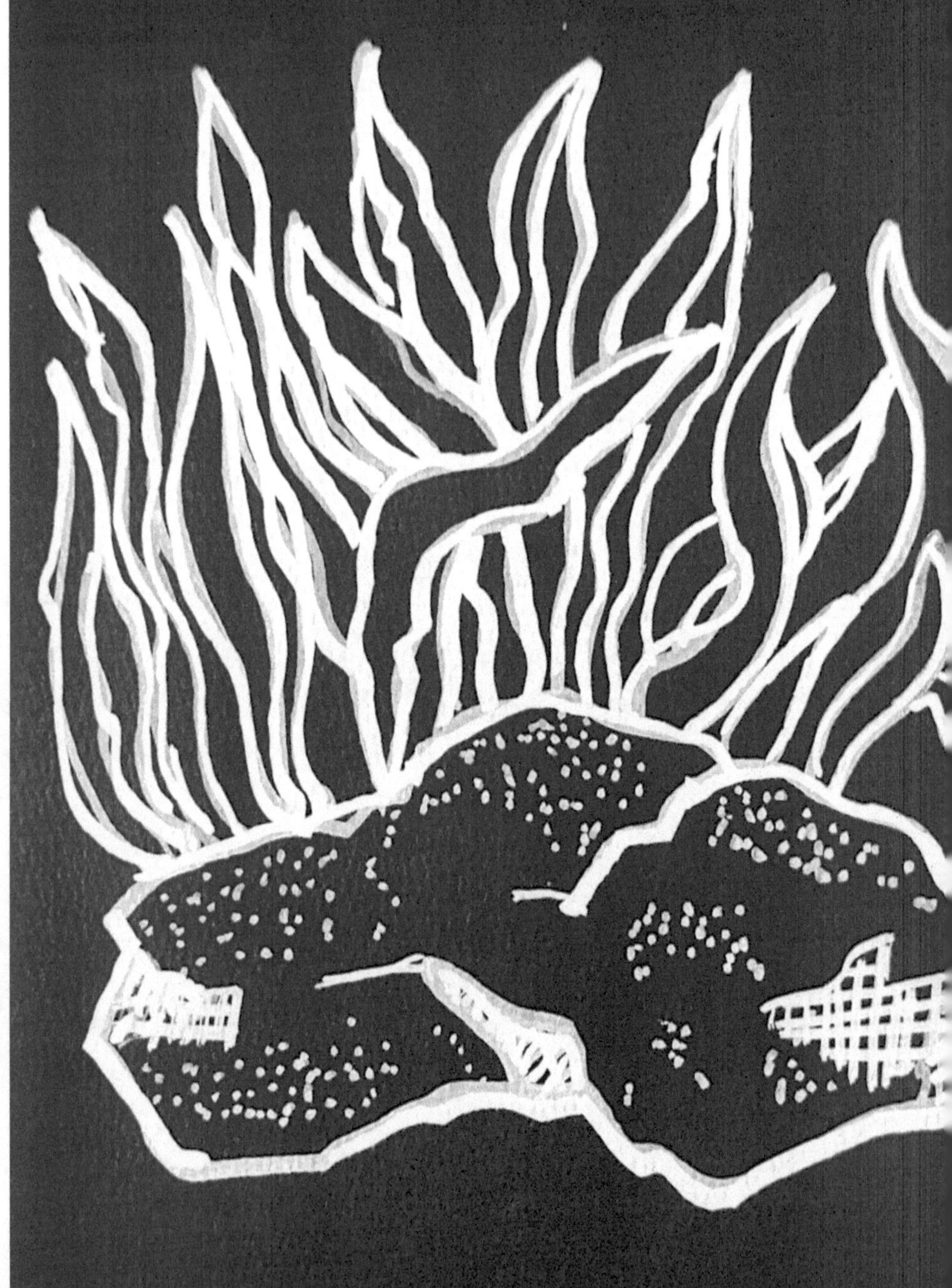

Grass growing out of rock.
Unexpected.
All your needs are met.

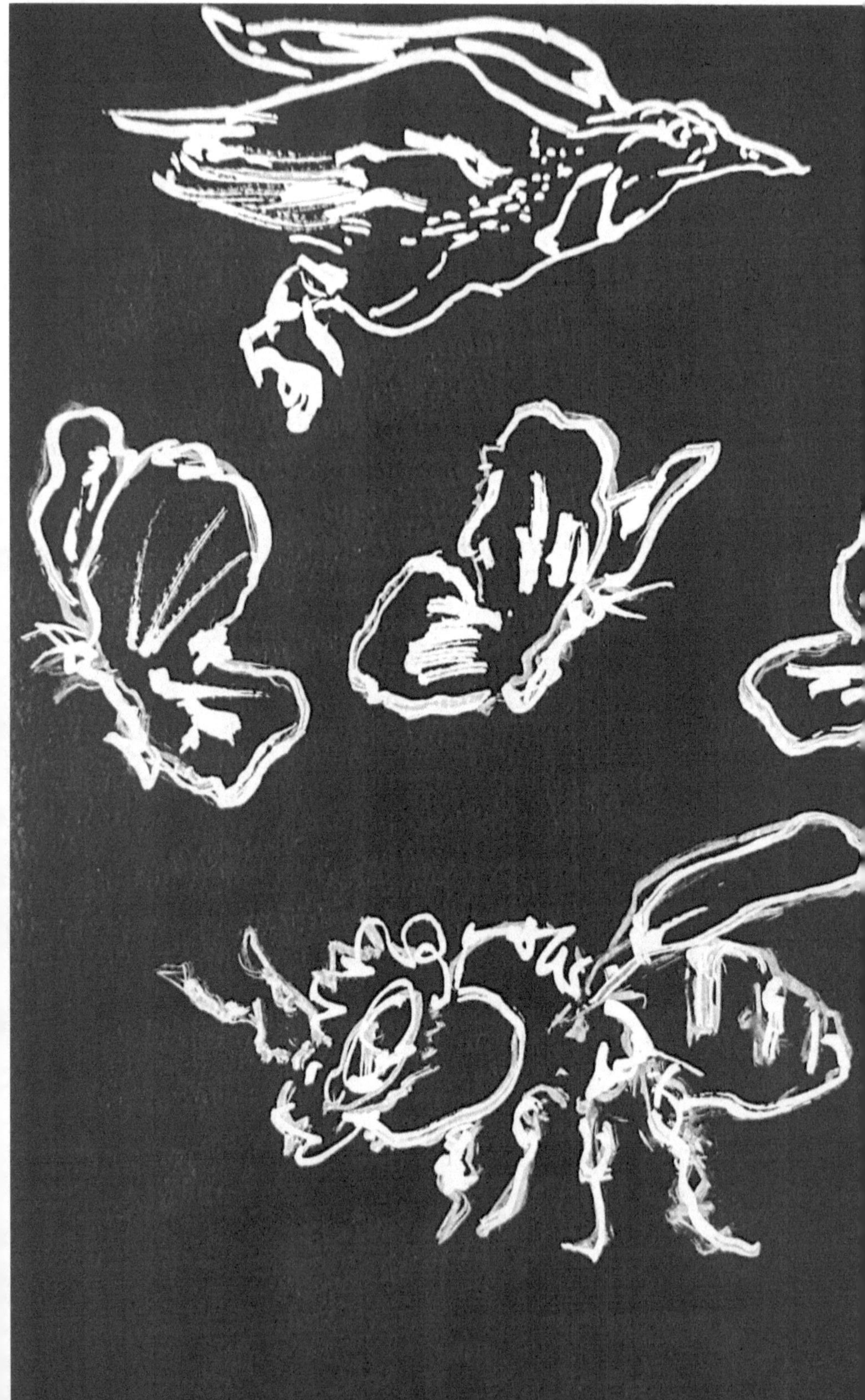

How taxing it must be
for butterflies to fight the wind!
Strong birds above
and fat bees below
have no sympathy.

May I offer you a ride
in the shelter of my cupped hands?
You're just as new
as me, and we're figuring
it out together.

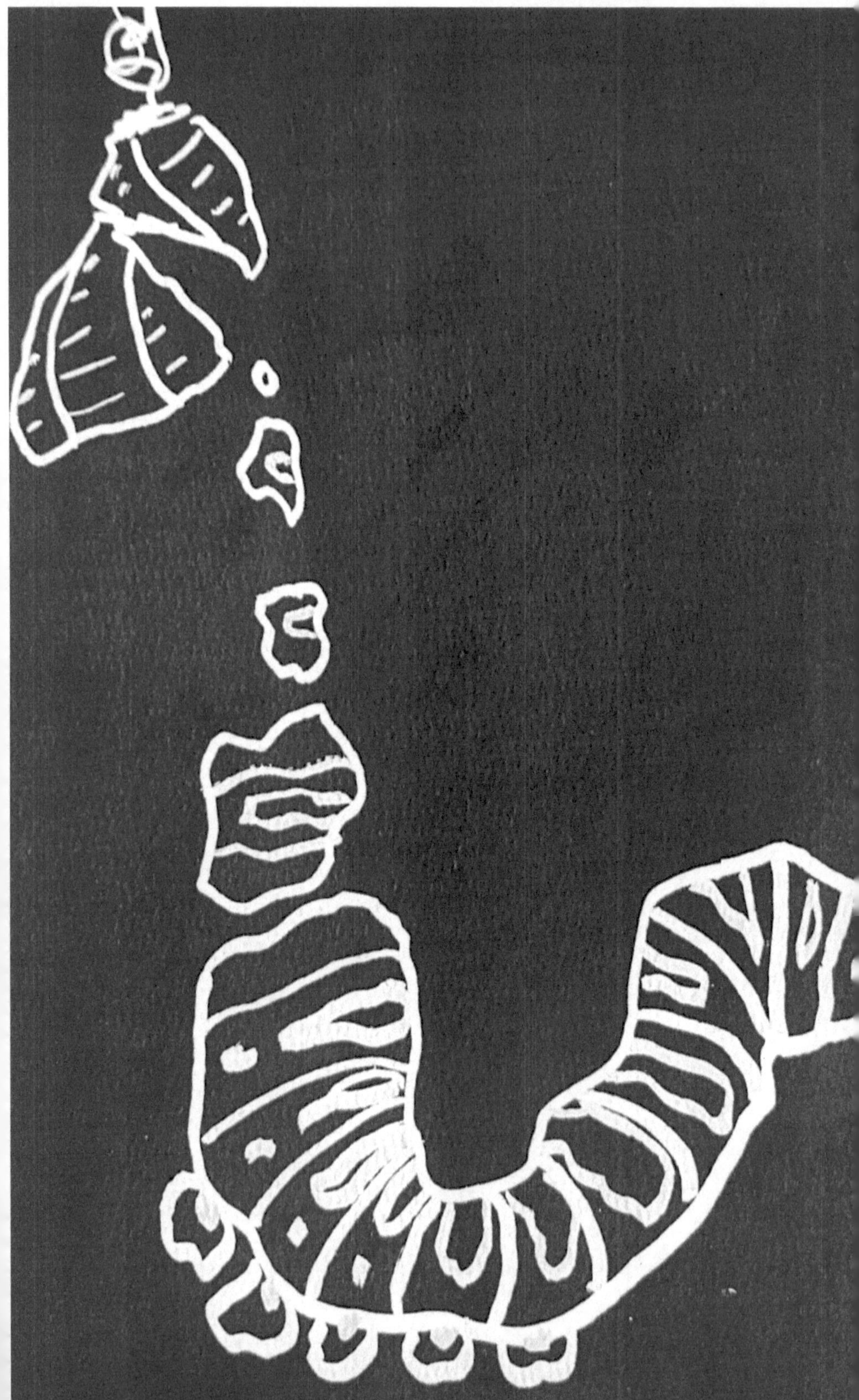

All creatures love
the soft hair of the tallgrass,

so I shouldn't have been surprised
when, while petting it, my fingers snagged
a cocoon. For a moment, I stared
at the perfect pod in my hand, shocked
at the thought of the puddle of caterpillar
becoming a butterfly in there, terrified
I ruined its metamorphosis.

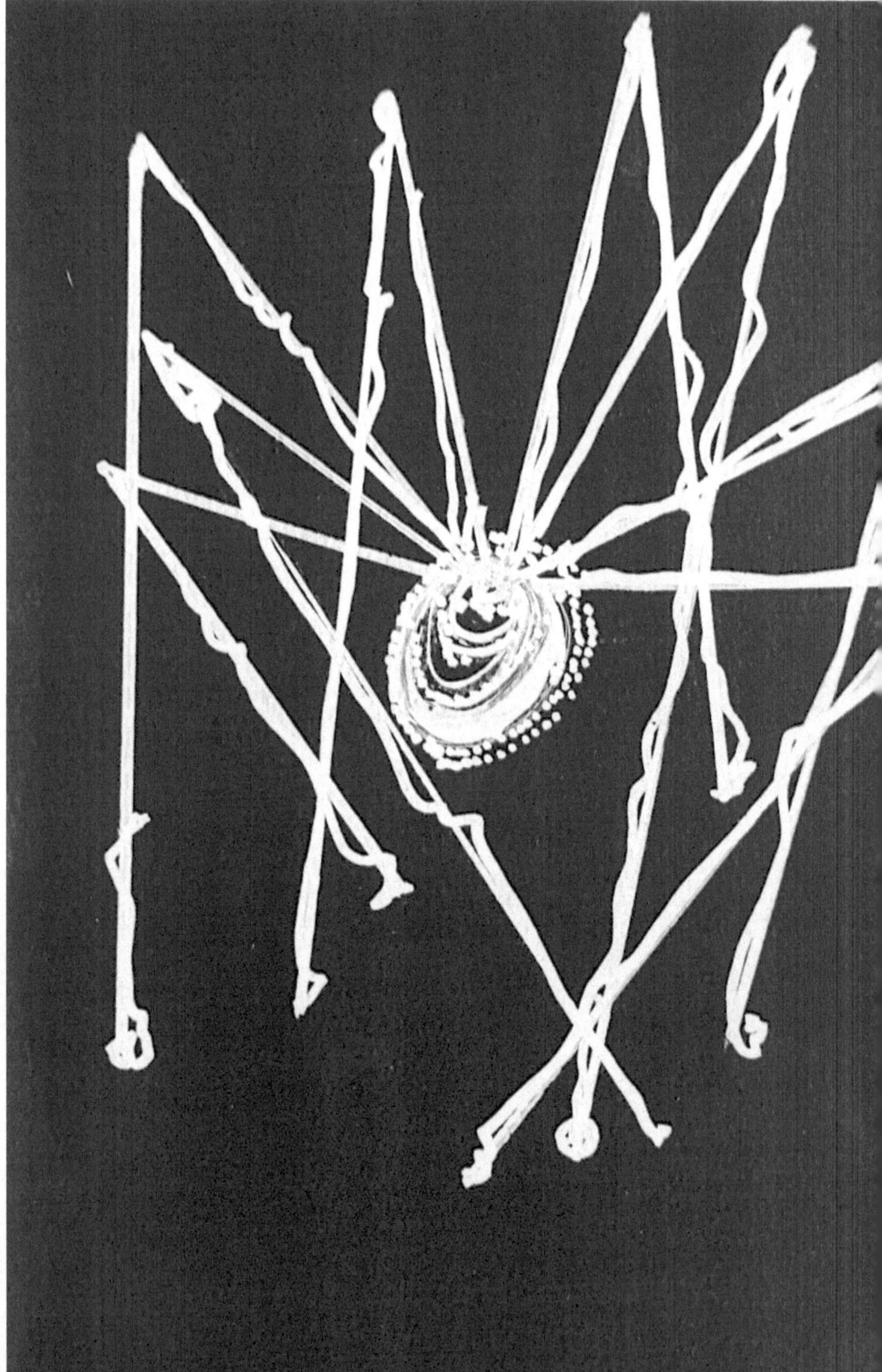

Daddy long-legs,
so elegant and light.
I bet you're a real good dancer.

In the pile of fallen leaves,
you suck on summer's carcasses.
Still hungry, you move on.

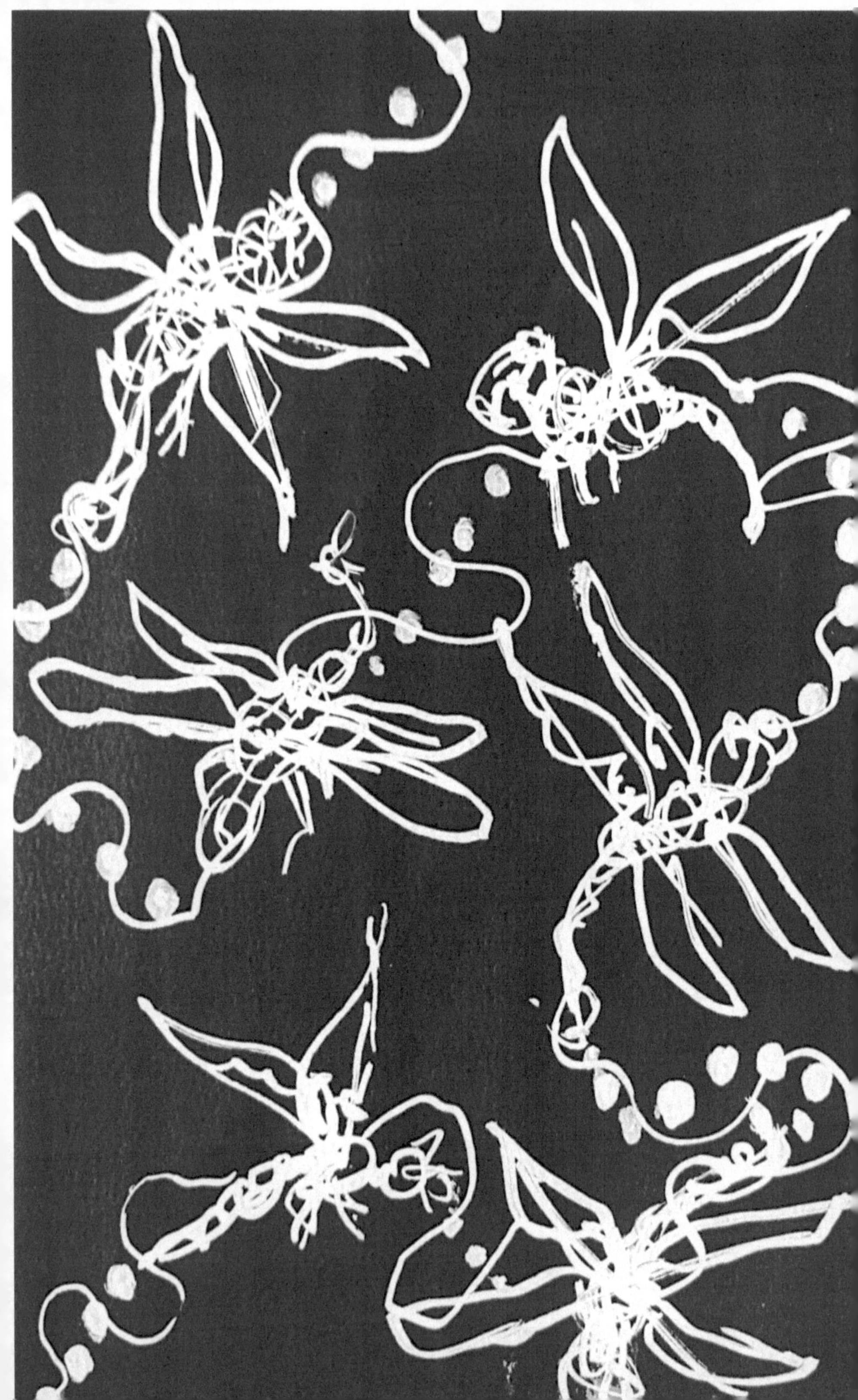

The drunk dragonfly
crashed into my shoulder,
but I'm the one who said,
Pardon me.

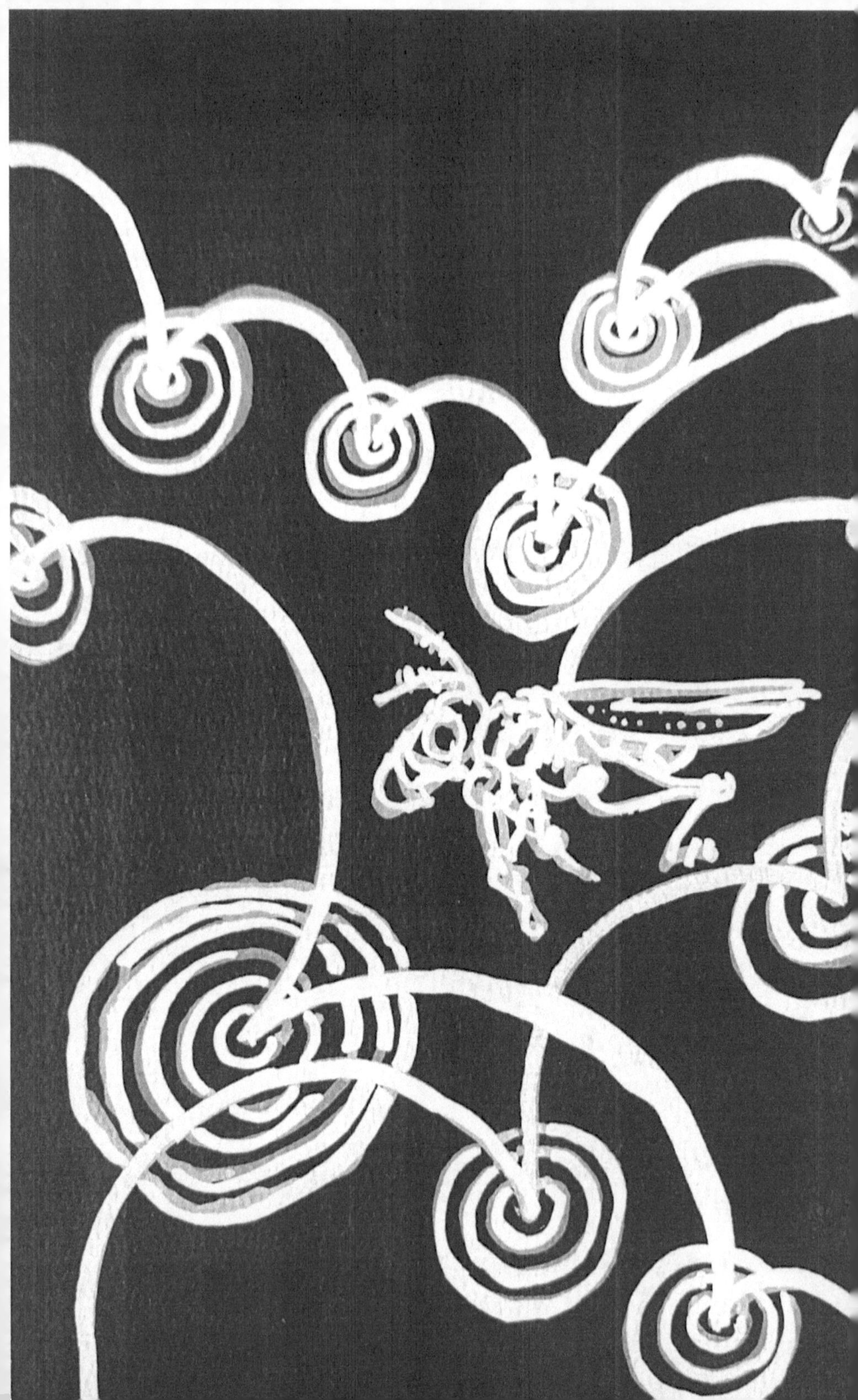

There it is—
the grasshoppers' playground!
I am ready
to play!

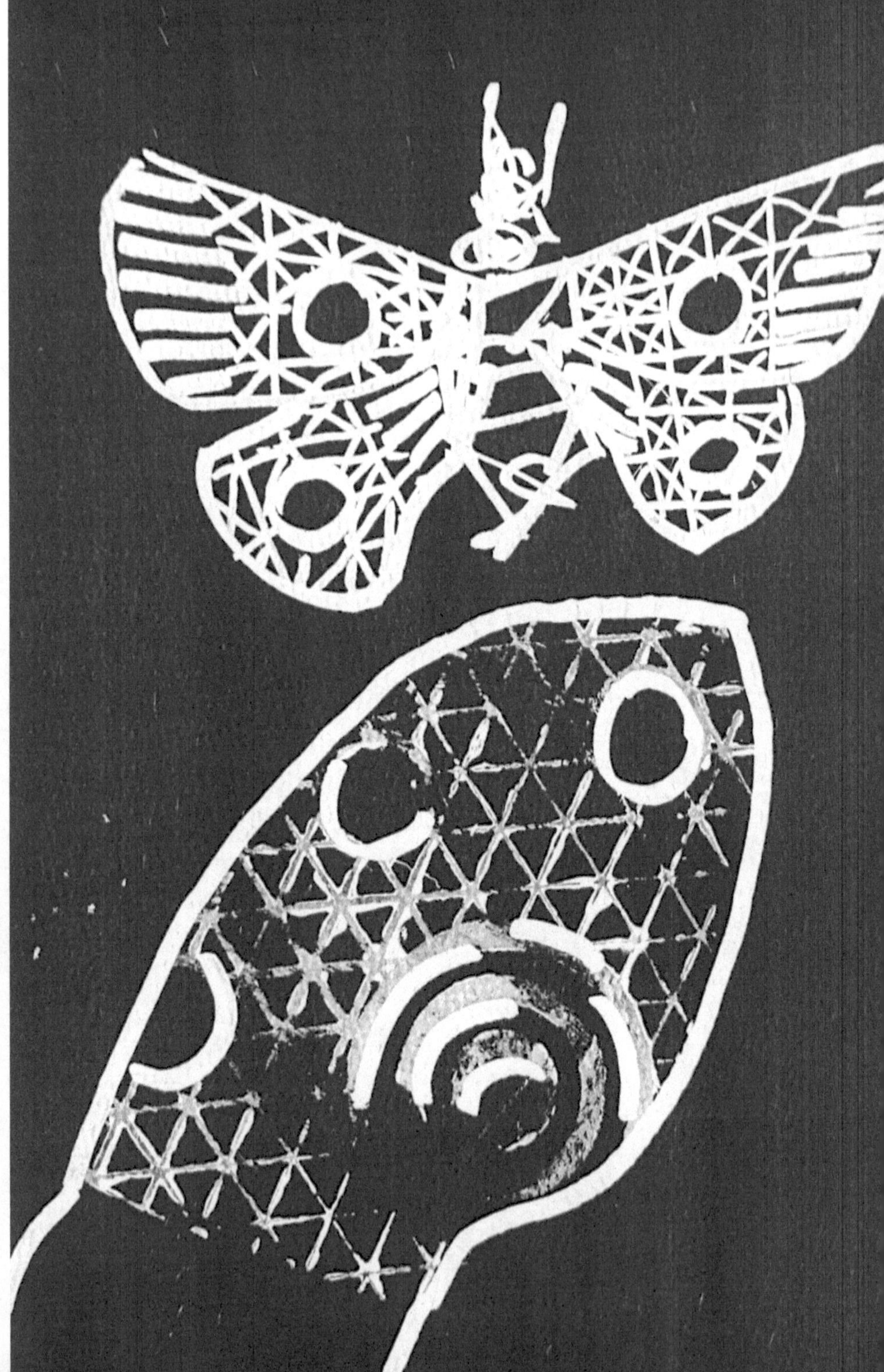

Moth,
I thought you were a leaf.
Thank you
for flying away before
I stepped on you—
an autumn crunch
I didn't want to make.

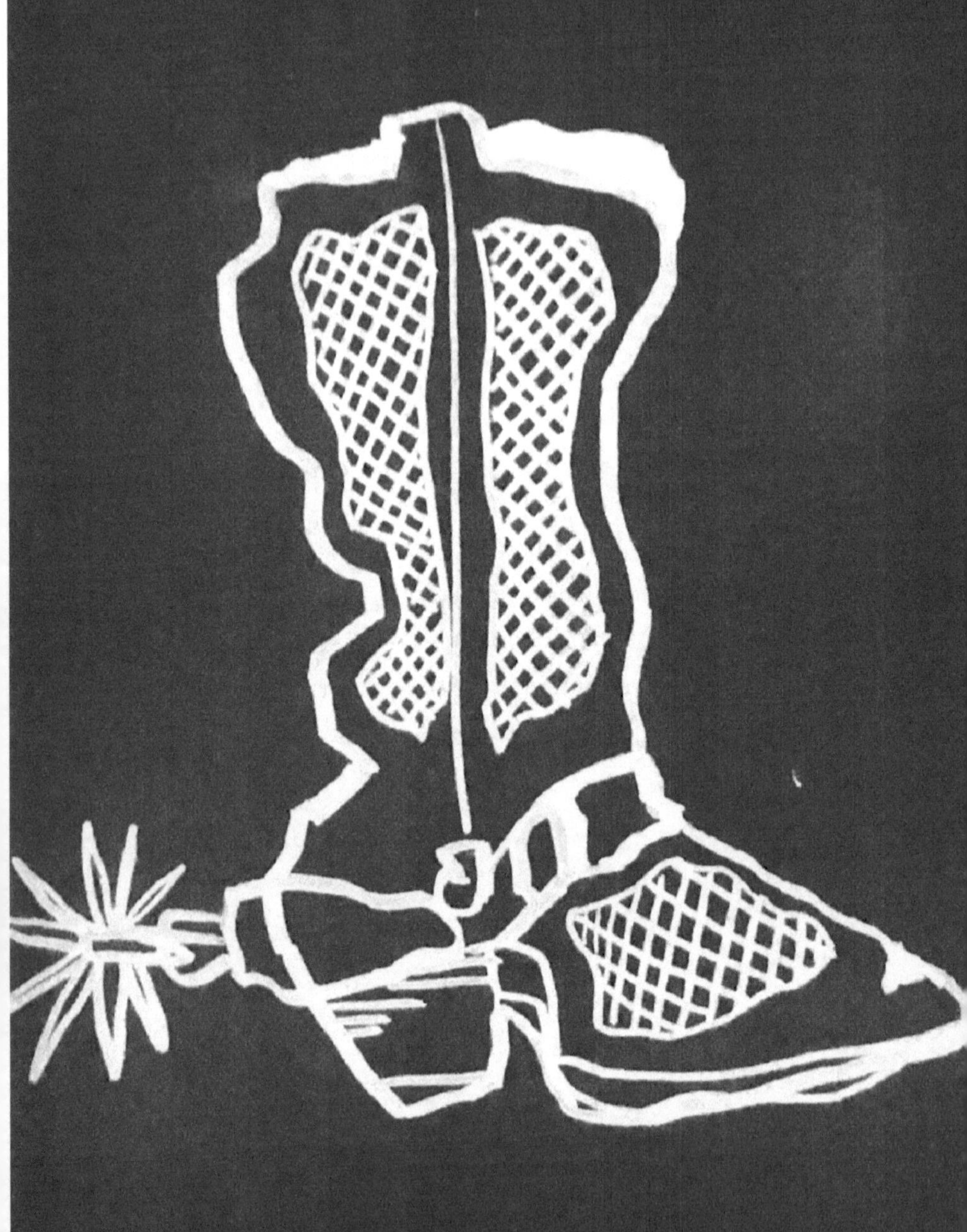

At the horse stable,

Rule #1:

Have fun by obeying

the Wranglers.

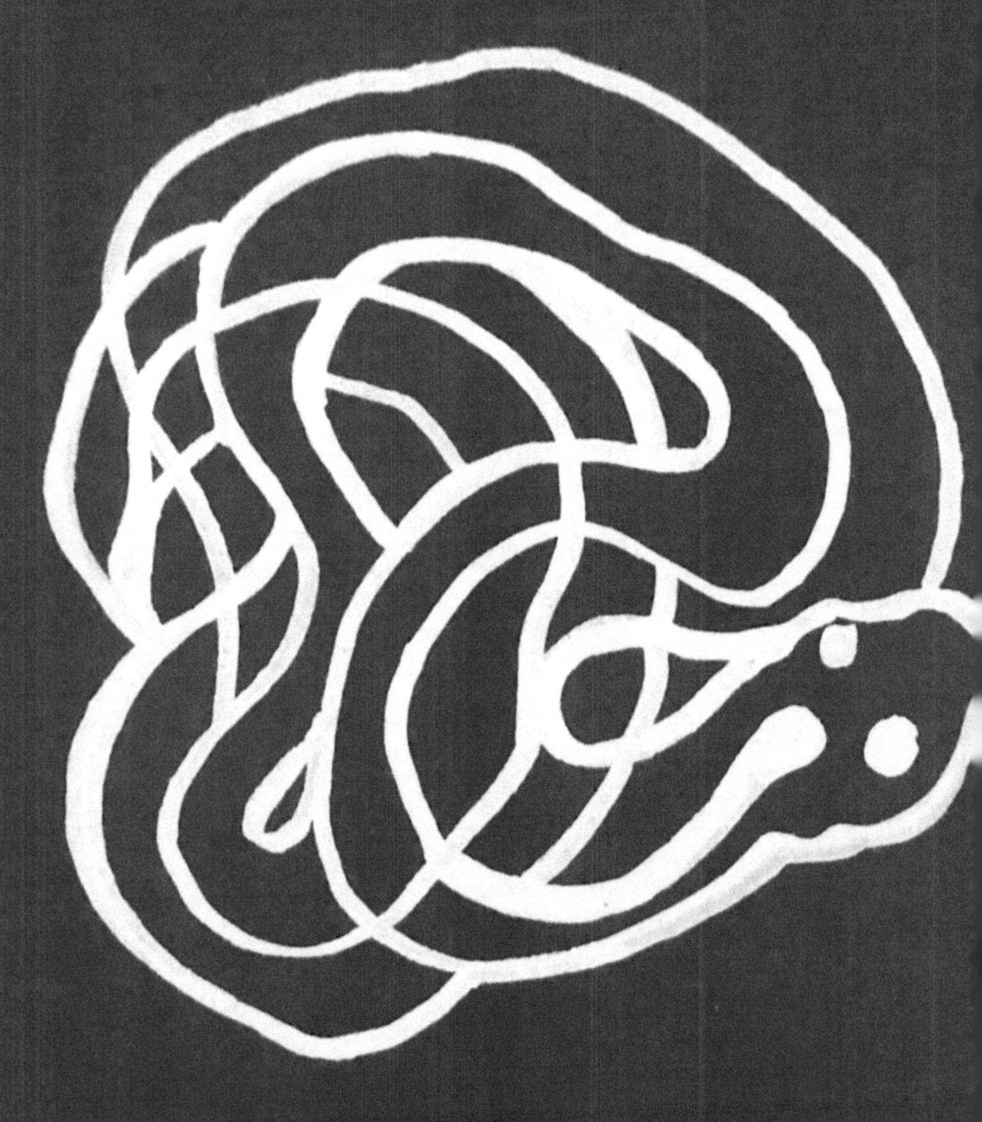

I walked right into
a snake's home,
stepped right in
the hole without knocking—
no wonder I got bit.

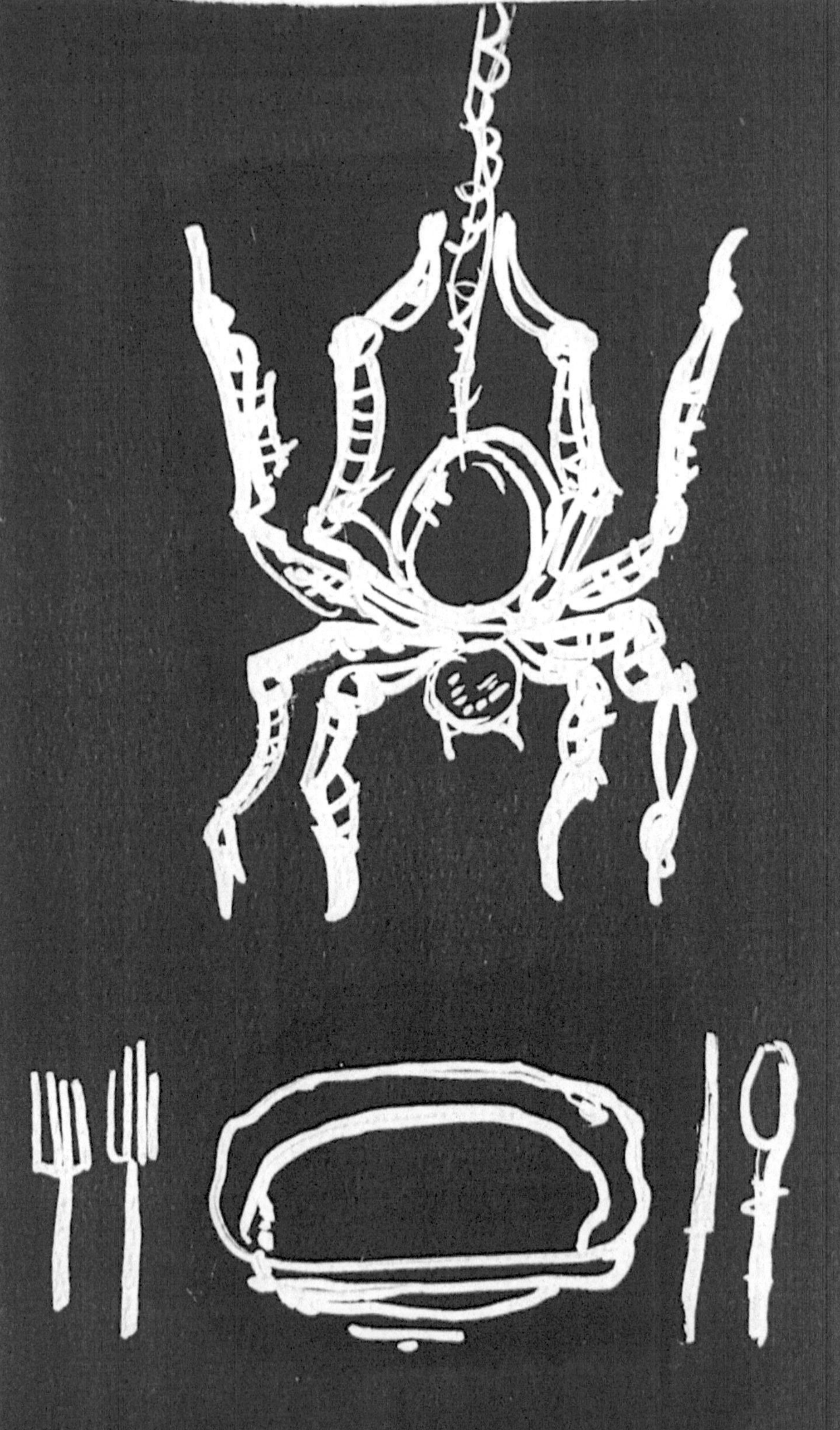

Spider,
your
web
got
caught
in my hair. I'm sorry
I stole your dinner.
I'm sorry
you'll have to start
from scratch.

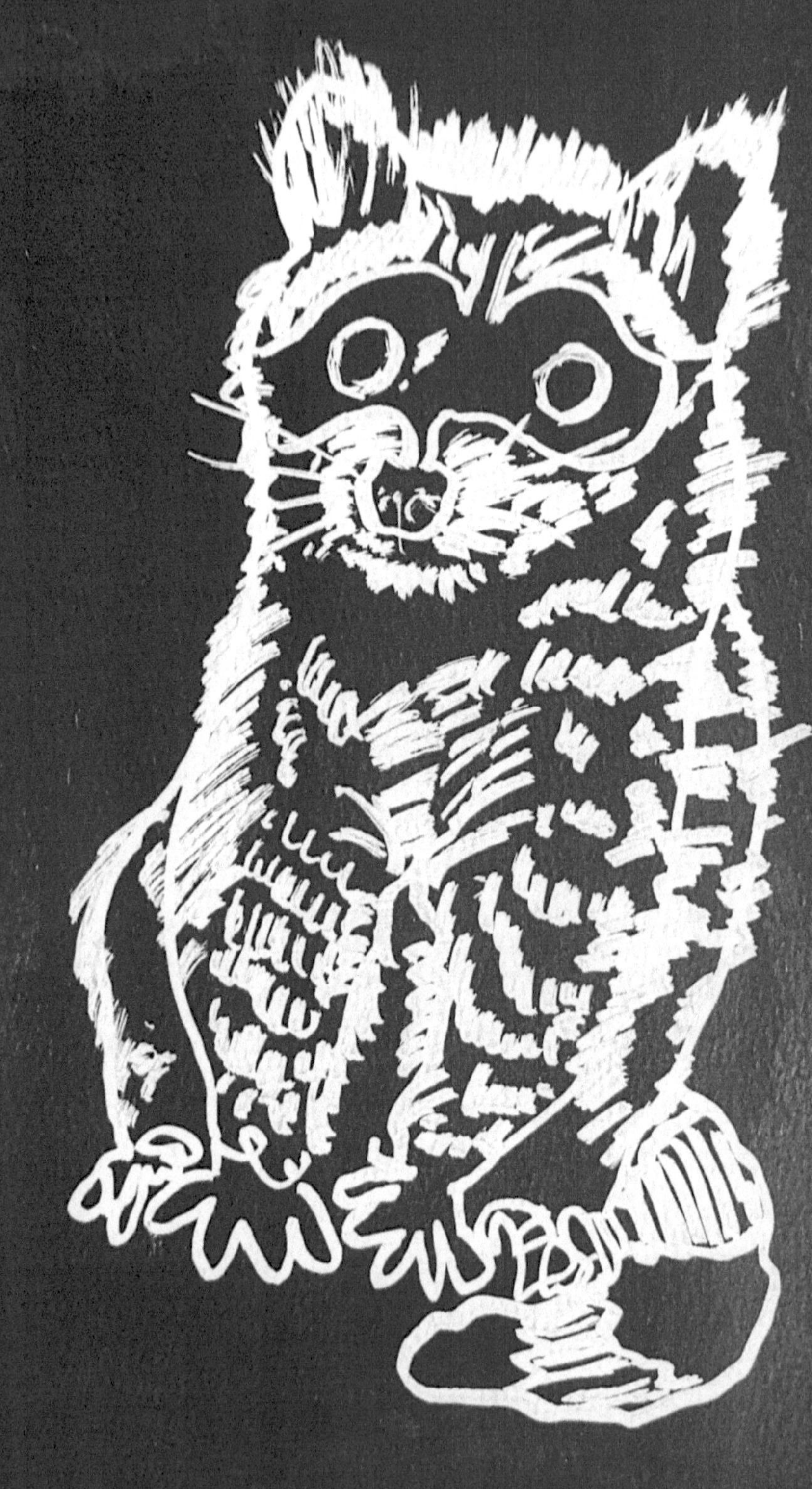

Young racoon,
little racoon,
under the bridge,
you look embarrassed
that I found you
so easily, like I joined
a game of hide and seek
I wasn't invited to.

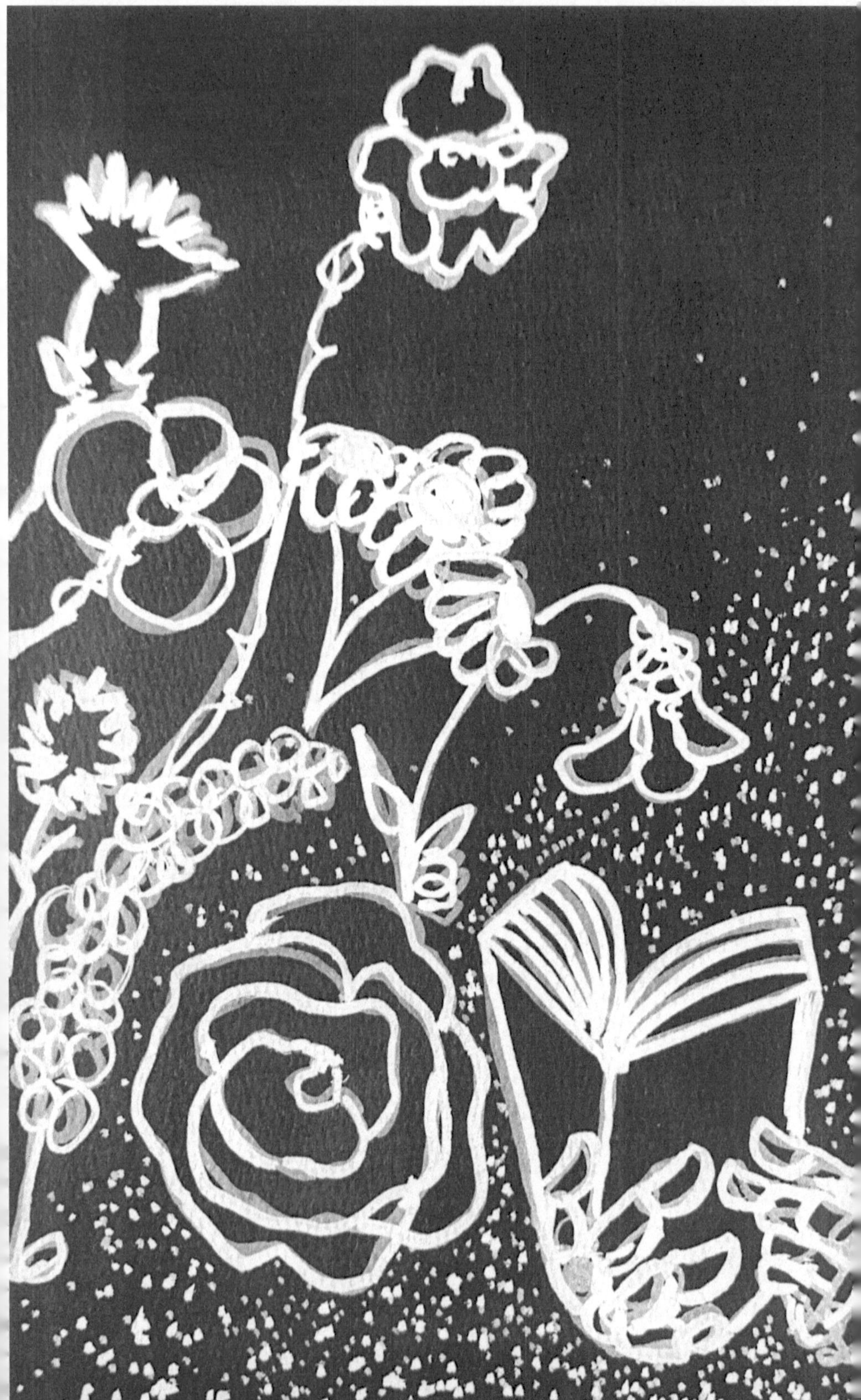

Wildflowers,
take a break.
You've done enough
for the poets today.

Relax,
I'll read to you.

Would you like to hear
what I wrote about
your good taste and
the sunshine in your smile?

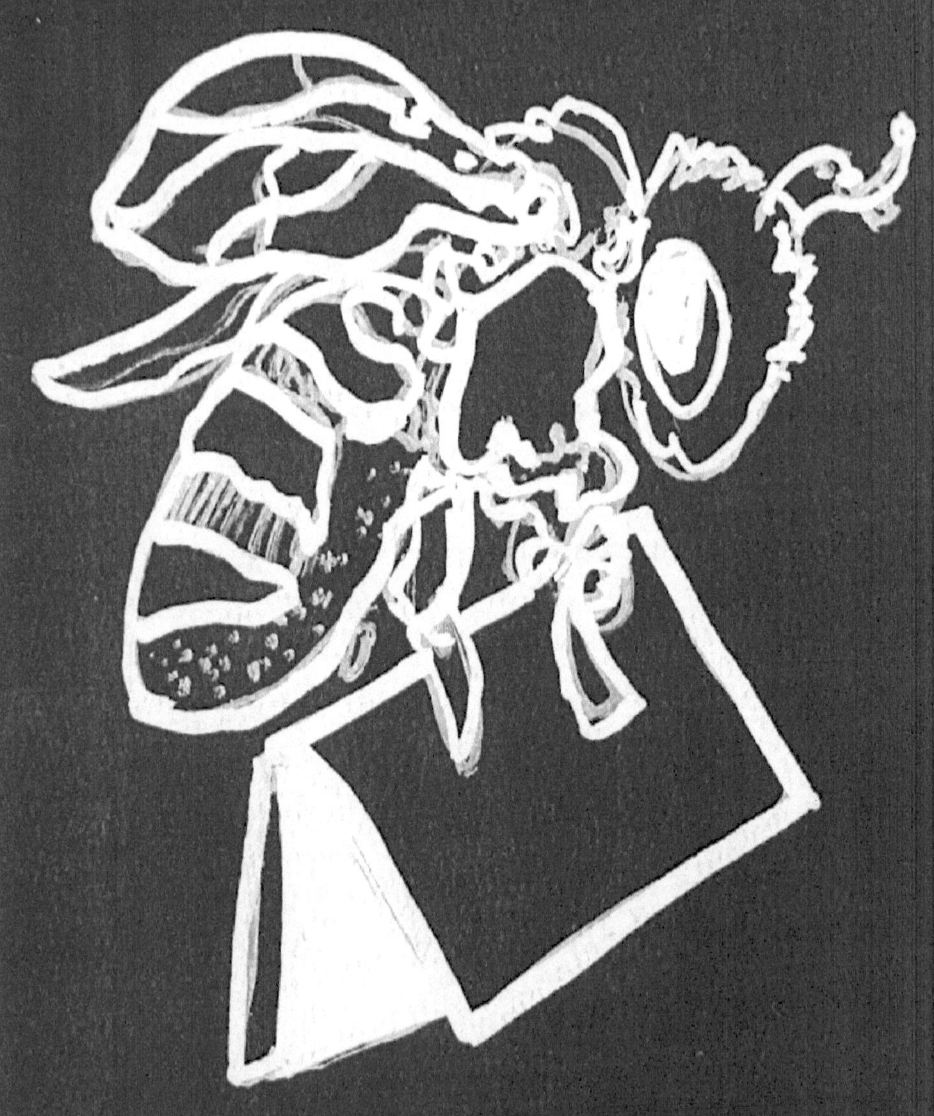

Bee on my page
trying to pollinate the flowers
I've just written about.
Don't you know better than that?
Don't you see the rose over there?

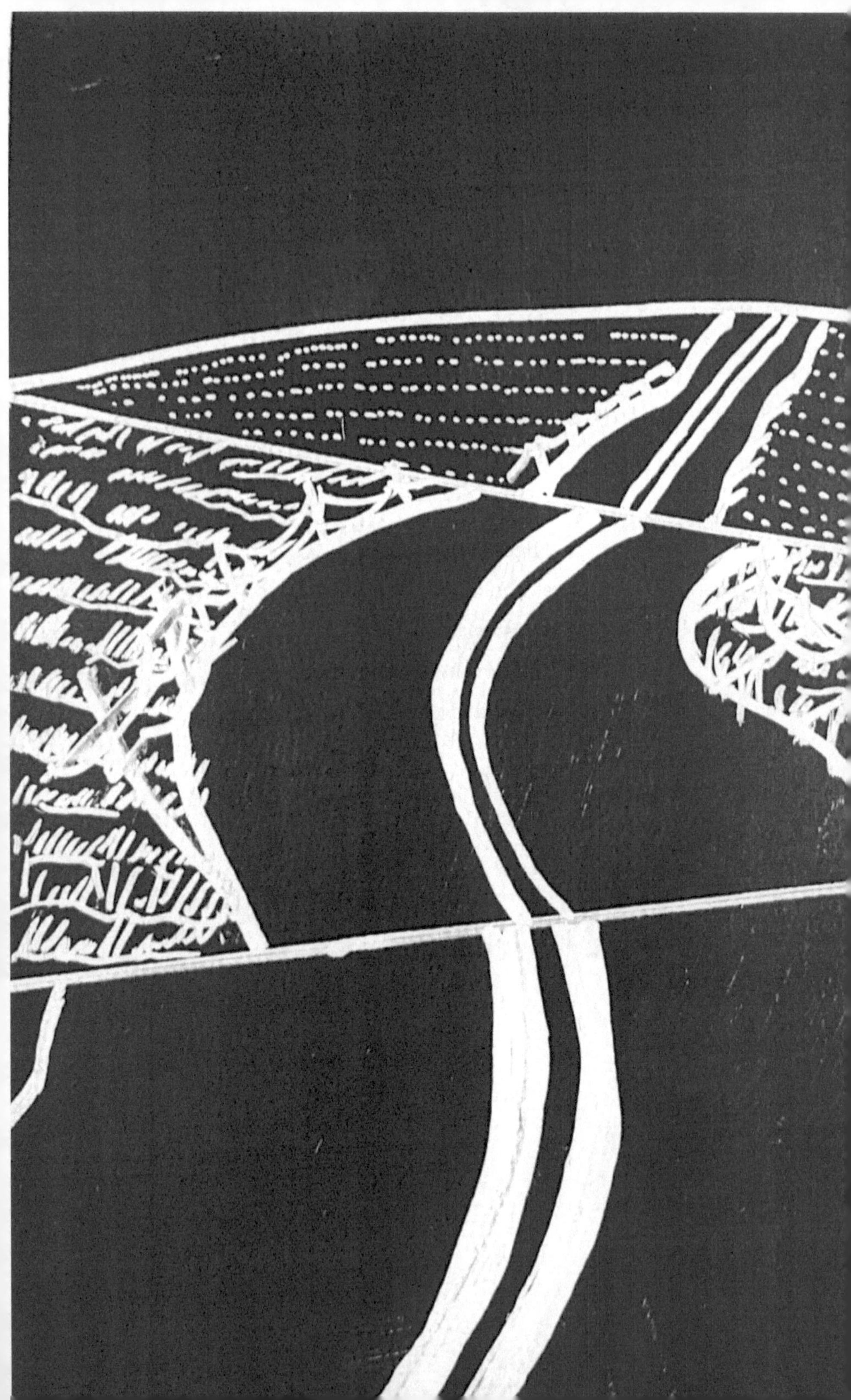

The trail turns into road,
and the road turns into more road,
and more road turns into hunting grounds,
and hunting grounds turn into the rest of the world.

This project was made possible, in part, by generous support from the Osage Arts Community.

Osage Arts Community provides temporary time, space and support for the creation of new artistic works in a retreat format, serving creative people of all kinds — visual artists, composers, poets, fiction and nonfiction writers. Located on a 152-acre farm in an isolated rural mountainside setting in Central Missouri and bordered by ¾ of a mile of the Gasconade River, OAC provides residencies to those working alone, as well as welcoming collaborative teams, offering living space and workspace in a country environment to emerging and mid-career artists. For more information, visit us at www.osageac.org

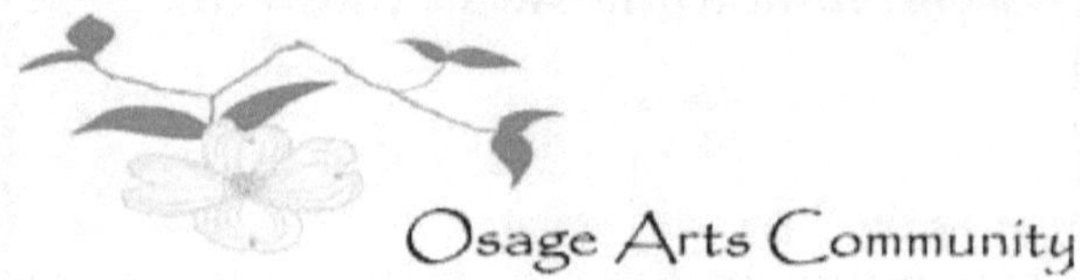

www.ingramcontent.com/pod-product-compliance
Lightning Source LLC
Chambersburg PA
CBHW051419130726
47989CB00007B/2996